I0080897

ISBN: 978-91-985174-1-5

Table of content

65+ tips on what to do as retired

Why do I write this book? I am not a retired. It is my recently retired parents who have inspired me to write this book, even if they do not know that. I just want them to be happy - and everyone else too that finally has come to that point of life when you do not work anymore.

The main target group for this book is "young retired people" - by that I mean people who just retired and might need some inspiration with what to do with all the time that you have longed for!

You are more than welcome to share your own tips and ideas among the comments at this blog: sixtyfive-plus. blogspot.com.

Have fun!

Chapter 01. Family and friends

OI.

Party

Organize a festive dinner, lunch or just a simple coffee rendezvous for your family. Invite to a party with no specific reason, set the table with your best porcelain and serve really good food and drinks to that.

Friends and family

O2.

Invite

Call a friend that you have not talked to for a long time, dare take the step and make that call, even if it was long time since last time or just send a text message. Both of you will surely be happy!

Friends and family

03.

Municipality arrangements

Check out what the municipality arranges for its elder citizens. Call or check out the website. You can often have lunch at the service center and residential homes and participate in activities organized there without living there. If you feel too young, you can go there and just have a good lunch and maybe some smalltalk.

Friends and family

04.

Local associations and clubs

Check local associations and clubs. There are a plenty of those, that organize meetings and excursions and other gatherings. Maybe there are new friends you have not met yet!

05.

Grandchildren

Invite the grandchildren for soda and sandwiches - without parents. Or invite the kids to sushi. Let them bring one of their friends too!

o6.

Write

Write anything. Write a cookbook
with your favorite recipes.
Document your knowledge that
you have collected over the years!
Maybe you end up as a writer in
the olden days!

Friends and family

O7.

Write your memoirs

Write down important milestones in your life to give to your children and grandchildren. Write important dates, addresses where you lived and for how long, what your schools you went to, in which church you got married, about vacations and places you've been to earlier in life. This can be very valuable to your younger relatives! Make a nice book as a gift and maybe several copies if you have many children and grandchildren and maybe even grandchildren.

There are websites that can help you on the paths with this, search for "keepsake grand-children".

o8.

Babysit other people's children

Offer to babysit other people's children, not just your own grand-children. It is a very welcome favor to many parents busy schedules.

09.

Stay in touch

Make sure not to lose contact with those who enrich your life. A short text message is good enough.

Set up a goal for yourself to have one social contact a day: by phone, mail or perhaps a handwritten postcard.

Friends and family

IO.

Find your family history

Maybe not completely unexpected, but it's so easy today when you can search online. When you come back to the 18th century, it is quite exciting. It might end with a family reunion somewhere in the world you have never been to.

Links:
www.genealogi.com
www.ancestry.com

Friends and family

II.

Start blogging

It is never too late to start blogging, 103+ years old Dagny in Sweden shows that! You may have relatives around the globe who would like to see how and what you are doing. You can set up your blog so that is is not public.

Links:
Dagny's blog: http://www.123min-sida.se/Bojan/ (in Swedish though, but still worth seeing!)

Chapter 02.
Activities

12.

Daytime activities

Look up daytime activities that suit you. It may be nice to have a fixed time each week to relate to, such as exercising or lunch dates.

Activities

13.

Take a course

Learn how Instagram works.
Learn Spanish.
Learn how to cook.
Learn to play the guitar.
Learn to paint with acrylic.

14.

Take morning walks

Bring coffee and go outside early as the sun rises and enjoy the silence. A new routine that you maybe did not see yourself doing before you retired?

15.

Start a study group

The good thing is that it can be about anything! It does not have to be about how to make lace or crosswords, it can be about how to brew your own beer including beer tasting or how to invest on the stock exchange with tips and advice to each other. It may be a discussion group or a book circle with themed authors from China.

16.

Stay cheap at hotels near home

On weekdays, many hotels have extra good rates on accommodations and packages.

Make a staycation - holiday at home.

Activities

17.

Travel!

Travel whenever you want. You do not need to wait for holidays when prices are extra high. You can also find a last minute trip. If you have specific requests like staying on the first floor, make sure to contact the hotel in advance, they will help you to solve your needs. Travel to warm places when it is not so hot. Or travel to the colder parts during the summer.

Activities

18.

Exchange houses for vacation

There are websites where you easily can become a member and temporarily change housing with others.

Example:
www.homeexchange.com
www.homelink.org

19.

Rent a mobile home

Be free and just drive where you feel.

20.

Senior discounts

There are a lot of clubs that have the only focus on negotiating good prices for everything from food to cars for the pretty large target group seniors which means good deals.

21.

Read

On tablets you can adjust the text size for your eyes. Read fiction. Read fact books. Read borrowed books. Read the books you exchanged in a book club.

Activities

22.

Grow a herb garden

Search for images of "herb garden" for inspiration. Then you can start planning or even start building, depending on the season. Keep in mind that you can use pots or build extra high cultivation boxes to avoid bending down.

23.

Pinterest

Learn how Pinterest works.
For example, save pictures on ideas
for gifts or places you want to go.

24.

Get a Facebook account

If you do not already have an account, then it's a great way to find old friends and colleagues and thus reconnect. You do not have to post anything online about you and your life. If nothing else just to keep in touch online.

Borrow a randomly selected book

Go to the library and let your gut feeling guide you: choose a random book and see if you find any interesting topic that you never even thought of reading.

Activities

26.

One activity outside the house or apartment per day

It's nice to come out and just see other people. You do not need to talk to anyone, but it's a bit energizing to see some hustle and bustle.

Activities

27.

Start an alumni association for former colleagues

Do you miss your job and your colleagues? Start an alumni association for those who previously worked on the same company.
It does not only have to be retired people: everyone who has worked together is welcome - nice with some age variation too.
Or check if there is one already.

28.

Get a pet

Get some company that makes you go out every day in the shape of a dog. A cat also works and is literally more self-propelled than a dog that needs to be walked. There are also fish, hamsters or rabbits that can join and create some work!

Activities

29.

Sign up for Netflix

Do like the youngsters: stay inside, even if the sun shines, and watch five episodes of the same series in a single day. Then you might also find some new energy to do things in real life too, although there are many good series...

3o.

Do unexpected things

Do something that amazes your-self or maybe even something that scares you a little bit.
Exactly what, only you know!

3I.

Bucket list

Create your list of things you want to do, places you want to see, dishes you want to try and check them off as you meet your goals.

32.

Winter swimming

You do not have to have a sauna for winter bathing. Warm and dry clothes and a thermos of coffee or tea are good enough. It is so refreshing with a quick dip in the blue waves.

Activities

33.

Plant a vegetable garden

Do some gardening and grow vegetables together with some friends: share the work and watering and it will be easier in the long run. Sharing is caring!

34.

Search for funds

There are huge amounts of money to apply for, even for individuals. Many foundations aim to support older people.
Search for "foundation" or "trust" on the internet. Note that the usage of the language sometimes might be oldfashioned!

35.

Feed the birds

Yes, you read correctly. Bring bread or seeds into the outdoor and feed the birds when it is cold and difficult for them to find food. Soothing. And you feel good when doing good.

And the birds by the pond get food anyway!

36.

Grow hydroponically

Grow lettuce and herbs indoors throughout the year. Simply search the web for "hydroponic cultivation".

37.

Instagramming

You may think blogging is not for you? Get an Instagram account and learn how to follow others, search for hashtags, and just the things you're interested in.

How do hashtags work on Instagram? Put this character: #, in front of a word, then it becomes a link that you can click on and see what other hashtag images are tagged at the same word.

Example: #william - anyone who tagged his image with "william" or check what's about #londonderry, #pinappleburgers or #spanners!

Activities

Chapter 03. Arrange and sort

38.

Clear out

Just keep those things that really matter to you. Or simply give them to someone, with the story of who you got it from, such as this candle-holder fromm the engagement party in 1964.

Arrange and sort

39.

Sell your stuff on flea markets

You will hopefully sell most of the stuff at the same day and not one at the time as if you sell on the internet. And an extra plus is that you will get some extra cash at the same time as doing a good deed for the environment reusing things.

Arrange and sort

40.

Clothes

Clean out the closet and get rid of old clothes that do not fit or that you never even used: give away or sell: learn how to sell online, such as Ebay or your local Facebook Marketplace.

Arrange and sort

41.

Photographs

Sort photos. Write on the back
what the subject is and also when
the picture was taken.

42.

Pick rubbish

In Sweden there is a movement called "plogging": picking up trash while jogging. But you can walk and pick up rubbish. Have a bag when walking in the woods or along the beach and picking up what trash you find and can pick up. Feels good!

Arrange and sort

43

Get the perfect garage

Clean out and sort the garage. Give away or sell duplicates of tools and arrange the keepgadgets nicely.

Arrange and sort

44.

Clear out
the whole house

Read about the Kon Marie-method online or buy the book. Marie Kondo from Japan is writing about how to systematically clean and sort in your home and life. It is based on the fact that one's things should glitter: then it is a keeper and keep all the stuff of one sort at the same place in the house. Harmony at home! It works for everyone, but most do not have time to complete it!

Arrange and sort

Chapter 04. Health and excercise

45.

Get the right gear and equipment

Make sure you have the right shoes if you want to walk a lot, maybe walking rods or a bicycle helmet if you ride your bike a lot (or once).

46.

Go to the gym

During the hours before lunch there are often mostly senior citizens at the gym. If you are a novice, you usually also have the right to an instructor for one or a couple of times.

You seldom regret going to the gym!

47.

Go for a walk

Put on comfortable clothes and go out for a walk, walk the same walk for a few times and measure if your time improves! Or bring a friend or a good audiobook to listen to and just enjoy your surroundings.

Health and excercise

48.

Water fitness

It is good for everyone and is not as burdening to the as walking.

49.

Ride your bike

Snap your helmet, go for a ride on your bike and make it a habit to get away with the bike for an hour a few days a week. You will probably appreciate the shifts in weather, light and seasons - and also to see people with the same habits and routines as you.

50.

Senior training

Check out the tennis club, the badminton club or the swimming club if they have classes specially adapted for seniors.

5I.

Try a yoga class

Everyone can try yoga and even if you are a beginner you will get something out of of the first class. You stay at the same place all the time during the class and do not have to worry about moving to the left when everyone else moving to the right. You do not even have to wear tight gym wear. You can often try once for free.

Health and excercise

52.

Do a health test

Make a reservation at the health center and take a health test - and do it regularly: once a year!

53.

Diets

There is no ultimate diet. On the other hand, much research have been done and trends come and go. Read about, for example, LCHF (Low Fat High Carb) if you happen to have a few extra pound or kilos (depending on where in the world you live!) and what it might mean to you to change your lifestyle.

Health and excercise

Chapter 05.

Eat and drink

54·

Start a dinner club

Cook a lot of food and have dinner with friends. Cook so much food so that you all can bring it home for lunch the next day. Next week or month you cook at someone's home.

Eat and drink

55.

Cook a three course meal in the middle of the week together

Divide the dishes and tasks between you but cook together. Set the table nicely and dress up for a very nice evening. Have a theme like 50's food, Italian food or maybe a Nobel dinner in the middle of December. The menus from last year's Nobel dinner can be found online and inspired by.

56.

Monday coffee

Go to the cafe every Monday at ten o'clock. Have coffee at the cafés in town. Or at home with each other!

57.

Bake

Bake bread and buns, learn how to make sourdough bread or taco shells.

Chapter 06.

Jobs and economics

58.

Review your finances

You've probably (and hopefully!) done it before, but put your numbers into an Excel document and try out a few different options with expenses, to see how much you have to deal with. It is easy to work with, but if you need you can can ask someone to help you set it up.

59.

Review your agreements

You may have been a customer for so long that you can call the company and ask if they have a better offer for you? It is worth the phone call! It may be time to change mobile subscriptions as well.

60.

Watch a dog

Getting your own dog can mean
more care than you want and
can handle. Therefore, walking
a neighbour's dog one or two
times a week may when they are
at work or someone who advertises
after a dog walker.
Post a request to Facebook or post
a note on the advertisement board
in your supermarket.

6I.

House sit

Watch the neighbor's house during their holidays. Or post an ad on local online advertising boards that you offer this service - and maybe even watch a dog or cat?

62.

Check out retirement job

There are companies specializing in just the job for retirees.

63.

Move

Move to smaller housing: fewer areas to clean, maybe a smaller garden and, above all: lower costs and money left over to others funnier things than bills.

64.

Rent your house

Rent your house or apartment while being away - it can finance a part of your trip! Check with the landlord so that is okay to do so.

65

Homework help

Are you a former Spanish teacher? Offer help with homework by the hour, either at your home or you will come to your student's house.

66.

Pick up children at daycare

Offer to pick up the children from kindergarten. Walk them home or go by car. It does not have to be more than that: it's still worth so much to parents. Pick up your own grandchildren or your neighbor's child.

Jobs and Economics

67.

And finally: relax

Allow yourself to enjoy the moment.

Have fun!

www.ingramcontent.com/pod-product-compliance
Lightning Source LLC
LaVergne TN
LVHW052037080426
835513LV00018B/2369